Advance Praise for *Starving Romantic*

Perrone's poems brilliantly crack open the wheezy engine that drives so many of our desires to journey toward homes both real and implied, metaphorical and visceral, dreamed and invoked. In this cracking open, Perrone reveals such an electric disappointment, the dependence of longing on close examination, and a seized, if still revivable, Midwestern kind of heart.

- Matthew Gavin Frank, author of
The Mad Feast and *Preparing the Ghost*

Starving Romantic is a brilliant debut. A meditation on finitude, contingency, and desire, the personae are caught between Greyhound bus stops in a landscape of doubt. Restless, unattached, yet self-possessed and wise, the voices that emerge in the poems are resolute. Like Michigan weather, we can't know our internal seasons, either, but it is "good / to be/ anything at all."

- Caroline Maun, author of
The Sleeping and *What Remains*

Vincent James Perrone's first book *Starving Romantic* is a major poetry debut from this young Detroit poet. With the earthy heart of Philip Levine and the inventiveness in language and form of e e cummings, this book is a treasure to behold.

- M.L. Liebler, author of
the award winning *I Want to Be Once*

These are beautiful, real-life poems in language that's just the right amount of music and horror, a set of dream poems and surreal memories and desires from the raw, present moment.

- Douglas Cole, author of
Bali Poems and Western Dream

Vincent James Perrone's *Starving Romantic* time and again tilts the world on its axis, investigates the degree of said tilt, and then with precision offers to the reader moments that are at once universal and intimate. This collection did much more than make the romantic in me starve—it fed my sense of exploration.

- Garrett Dennert, author of
Wounded Tongue

Starving Romantic is a brief confrontation with mirror images. These poems confront their own memories and melodramas, examining the function of longing and how it affects the soul. Perrone expertly evokes the language of nostalgia.

- Mike Corrao, author of
Man, Oh Man!

STARVING ROMANTIC

Starving Romantic

BY

VINCENT JAMES PERRONE

STARVING ROMANTIC

Copyright © 2018 by Vincent James Perrone

All rights reserved.

This book may not be reproduced in whole or in part, except for the inclusion of brief quotations in a review, without permission in writing from the author or publisher. No part of this publication may be reproduced, stored in or introduced into retrieval system, or transmitted, in any form, or by any means (electronic, mechanical, photocopying, recording, or otherwise), without prior permission of the publisher. Requests for permission should be directed to 1111@1111press.com, or mailed to 11:11 Press LLC, 4757 15th Ave S., Minneapolis, MN 55407

Library of Congress Control Numbers: 2018944552
ISBNs: 978-1-948687-03-4 (paperback), 978-1-948687-02-7 (ebook)

Cover art: "Force Fed" © Zoe Beaudry is used with permission
Author photo by Evans Tasiopoulos

FIRST AMERICAN EDITION

Printed in the United States of America
9 8 7 6 5 4 3

For no one

                                          els*e*

CONTENTS

I | 13

Arrangements

Motion Sickness • 15
Holiday Shopping • 16
Michigan Weather • 18
Outside the Airport • 19
Just Asleep • 20
A Short Ride • 22
Late Funeral • 24
Cadillac • 25
Painting of a Cactus • 26
Arrangements • 27
The Unwatched Pot • 29
The Grind • 30
The Landing • 31
Underripe • 33
Visit • 34

II | 37

Bloom

Other Seasons • 39
On Waking • 41
Blond • 42
Requiem • 43
Bridesmaid • 44
Doe Eyes • 46
Sudden Illusion • 47
I Wish You The Best • 48
Our Garden • 49
Mythology • 50
Madrid to Detroit • 51
Space • 53
Cinema • 54
I Told You So • 55
Barbs • 56

III | 59

Memory Revisions

Lost Rivers • 61
Dinner Time • 62
Baby Teeth • 63
Weekends • 65
Fiddlestick • 68
Underpinnings • 69
Funnel Vision • 71
Agoraphobe • 72
Summer Sick • 73
Rust Belt • 74
Powwow • 75
Cloudbuster • 76
Fodder • 77
Animals • 78
A Curious Child • 79
Grand Rapids, MI • 81
Cardinal Direction • 83
Fortune Telling • 84
Thoughts on Time • 85

I.

Arrangements

"Our history is an aggregate of last moments"

—Thomas Pynchon

Motion Sickness

The dry heave
of a crowded Greyhound.
I'm not whispering
    just exhaling
    sheep.

A brunette leans a cheek
on bulletproof glass—
    eyes rolling gracefully.

I finger a ticket stub—
    feeling born
    and bred
in sheep's clothes.

If she's late
    I'll survey the parking lot
and stretch and groan and molt
      —eyeing the icicles.

Between Rosa Parks and Wealthy
the sun sets on French braids.
    I undo her hair
    and exaggerate the rest.
Sleep next to a warm body
or heat vent.

I look out the window
    to find
a hummingbird with a knotted throat
    croaking on a stop sign

    —to find
my compass
    cracked and stuttered.

Holiday Shopping

A quarter clogs a fountain
    in a small town American mall.

A boy picks his gold fillings
    and points to the food court.

I cut off the crust
    of the Midwest. He pouts
    hungry for more.

    He asks me a question—
something ugly
    that would scare his parents.

I flaunt the answer above his head.
    Grow roots
    lift your limbs
    and wait to bud.

The boy's too short
    to grasp it.

He beats me like a ripe piñata.
    I spill candy down his throat—
happy birthday.

You should've thrown a penny.
    You can't have 25 wishes.

When I was young
    the mall was
a fluorescent labyrinth

and my parents
    were minotaurs.
When I was young

I happily watched
    the tides
of the wishing well.

Now—a boy wraps a strand
    of Christmas lights
around my neck.

I feel joyous and full
    of blue-fevered spirit.

I told you I'd be home
    for the holidays.

Michigan Weather

Someone recites the forecast.
I hear and count ants
in September sun.

I wonder how much
dirt they carry
and if it ever feels
like enough.

I look for faces
but find rooms for rent.

I pause for a storm
on a porch
and know some brief serenity.

I remember Spanish moss
on old white brick.

People walk by
or I walk by them.
Each more beautiful
than the next—
none sure
what season it is.

Voices fall
toward me—through me
like a fill light.

The perennials bloom
and grow over my eyes.

We all bleed the quiet wind.
Things come and then go
and are rarely missed.

Outside the Airport

It was a country style rant.
Her hair pulled back
in a bun like an ostrich egg.
She bit her nails and they hung
ever so dearly.

The house was driving her crazy.
The wine rack crept
like a shadow.
She moved furniture
in the dead of night.

Her coffin
was more spacious.

In a country style diner—
outside the airport.
Cow-print placemats
and salt shaker like a hand grenade.
She spoke with strands of hair
that shimmered in greasy light.

The planes deserved applause.
All the tourists were let go
and she vanished
toward a blemished runway.

Goodbye fair city.
A passenger gets a rise
from an in-flight movie.
It's back to the country
where fruit flies prefer flesh
and I prefer the simplicity
of plucking violets
from her prepaid grave.

Just Asleep

Hungover on the swings
    you learned to jump from.
First attempt to borrow
    then purchase nostalgia.

Rock back against
    the tide of wood chips.
Watch the parade
    of sour-mouthed children.

Rest and digest
    a queasy dream.
Last night and every one
    before it.

You see the spoils
    of scraped knees.
A girl spins the wheel
    of a plywood car.

Her father rolls his sleeves—
    a crucifix on his forearm
and contorts
    into the passenger seat.

A boy grinds his cheek
    into a sandpaper slide.
He whistles the same lullaby
    that you forgot.

In the center
    of the park—
an elm tree with
    a dedication, "For Amy."

Amy—I wonder
     and wonder more are you
            just asleep
   under the shade of leaves.

Back at home you watch T.V.
     until your eyes blotch to
the shade
     of raw elbows.

On the swings
        in your mind—
you're nearly parallel
with the bar.

Chase the ring
     of the recess bell.
Everyday endless
     and without beginning.

Childhood is revered
     and exchanged. Now
you fight to negotiate
     the film rights.

A Short Ride

I.
A father and a father
before. A flower
curled around the clouds.
     It's good
    to be
homebound and restless.
Diving head first
  into crabgrass. Green
  in the back of a Greyhound.

Salt and smiles. Passengers
backwashed into paper cups
  of R&R and coffee.

    It's good
    to be
     anything at all.

An earring flung
  between the seats.
A woman with a cleft chin
presses her weight
  into my thigh.

II.

Fold your arms
  your legs.
Fold the corners of your mouth.
Fold your possessions
   into a single backpack.
Fold the ticket stub into your pocket.
Fold your hand and draw again.
  Fold the book

—dogeared for another day.
Fold the bus until it drips air conditioning.
Fold me into origami and leave me
        on the desk of a grade school sweetheart—
        I recall her arms
        folded around me.

Folded into memories
    and the coarse sleep
        of mass transit.

III.

It's good to be born
from ash. Fed ash.
Bleeding ash from trash cans
and gutters. Wherever
highways meet.

Prayers heard from the back of the bus—
three services a day. Lean
toward the road—white lines
recall your name.

My father picks me up—
Altoids rattle in his glovebox.
Mint middle class nausea.
He asks if that's what I'm wearing
to the funeral.

His father and father before
curled around his car keys.
A short ride home.
Shorter still.

Late Funeral

You don't need bobbers in this lake.

My grandfather and I used to fish
off the edge of the wide dock
near his white house.
Beware of dog
sign faded into carbon.

He was 95 years old
I counted his rings.

Hands
like I imagined God to have.
Fish don't feel pain.
I didn't believe him
but I hooked a bass
straight through its purple lip.

It thrashed on the blacktop.
Gills like tired eyes—
the smell trash and seagulls.

My grandfather—
hands on my shoulder blade
sharp with youth.

His breath
salt and oranges.
Our lures tangled
in green waves.

Green
waves.
Like a heart-rate monitor.
It all comes in waves.

Cadillac

For Matt

We are a must-see.

Garble of speaker heard
from the hood
of the Caddy—both hands
drunk and clubbing
the windshield. Subtle
new blood. A crane shot
off the back porch. Corn husk
in the gears of our finger.

If money could talk I'd translate.

A great slide across
the median. Swear you'd drive
blindfolded. Arms
crossed, legs buried
through the backseat(*slash*)road(*slash*)talk
that parallels the phone calls.

And then we're smiling over old men.

There's a roundness
to the dark. Something we know
in crushed decibels. A shared haunting
we could agree to.

Painting of a Cactus

For Jake

Maybe in Texas or Illinois
a stringy kid knew
the moon belonged
in the corner
of the canvas. Knew
that a cactus is black
when the sky is
orange and close
to yellow
at the base
of the horizon. It could be

in Philly that he doesn't
see that time
of day and puts palm
to knee to floor
posing for satellites
that pick up some desert
still buzzing
under his skin.

Another pose, both
arms raised, one
higher than the
other.
A saluting cactus.
Swift surrender
to a quarter-circle moon.

Arrangements

I heard the cat has six toes
on each paw. I heard the poem you wrote
was arranged in six sections but I've only seen two.
          She would go all day arranging wood chips at 90
          degree angles. Even under snow you'd see ridged
          ground. When I die I'd like to be a science class
          skeleton.
          She hasn't thought about it. My bookshelf is
          currently alphabetized but it should be separated by
          genre. I heard history is a line drawn and redrawn. I
          heard the woman next to me talking
          about Spain. I'll go there one day
          if only to upset someone. Now
          she's talking about France.

When I look at bricks I imagine them all
coming from the same place.
          I heard a properly placed mirror
          can really make the room feel bigger.
          When I cross a bridge I rarely think
          of what's in between. The dining room
          table is often covered in magazines, bottles,
          ash, paint brushes, elbows,
          candles, plates, and photographs of strangers
          with dirty hands. Four chairs circle
          like sharks.

          She always eats breakfast. I'm rarely
          awake for it. I like contrasts
          she doesn't find them
          nearly as interesting. I heard rain and
          opened my mouth.

There are spruce needles under the rug from
a tree I don't remember.
                I found a cradle
                by the dumpster. I heard
                a whistle through rough lips. I shivered a sonnet
                in need of a rewrite. There's a myth I'd never believe.

The Unwatched Pot

A young widow mourns
her wasted curves—
Fingers calloused from sewing baby clothes
that gather dust on her kitchen table.

A pot hums
unwatched
on her antique stove.
Lessons bubble over—
frothy wisdom seeps
like honey
from her nose.

She can see pine trees
from her stained glass windows
and she often rubs her knees admiring
the stillness.

She envies
that part of nature.
With the rest
she's unimpressed.

I wish I'd found her sooner.
Before she dropped the quilt
and threw the match.

Before the flames
licked the very top of her house
and the tiny sweaters
and tiny scarves
and hats made for tiny heads
were consumed
like hot applesauce.

The Grind

The laundry groans
below and I sleep
soundly through the afternoon.

Live paycheck to unpaid.
Check the mail
then the fridge
feast on overcooked noodles—
dog paddle
through zeros and ones.

Leaving the house
someone smiles at me
as I cross the freeway.

I wave back
with unexpected enthusiasm.
They turn away quickly.
They must've thought
I was going to jump.

The Landing

At the bottom of the stairs—
a puddle the color
of a dull penny
shaped like a miniature elephant.

The fireplace gives its last hiss
and a son reaches
for a father
who grinds maple leaves
into the welcome mat.

Between his mother's screams
he can hear the axis shift.

He kisses gravity
and gives his apology
counterclockwise.
Icarus at seven years old.

He grazes on stars—
churns galaxies
through his stomach.
A celestial bovine.

He lays in a puddle
the color of the welcome mat.
Leaves and earth and the soles
of his father's boots.

At the bottom of the stairs—
the son with a red crescent
on his skull.
That was new carpet.

His father holds a rag
to the fresh wound.
It all moves too fast
but he learns the word *concussion*.

He learns even more
at the bottom of the stairs.
The fragile lesson
of a fall just far enough.

Underripe

I never knew she wore dentures.

We shared a fear
of clogged sinks. On Sundays
we took drives—only six blocks
or so. She told me the best feelings
come from the pit
of the stomach and to only eat
underripe bananas.

She refused to be x-rayed
and continued to cut hair
in her basement.
The same customers
for fifty years. Last week

she looked swollen
as if she'd swallowed the moon.
There was a glow
from her throat
and blue veins
spiraled down her neck.

That week there was no drive.
We sat in her backyard
and her fingers were warm
when she laid them
on mine.

We watched the squirrels
dig up her hydrangeas
as the sun washed over
the vinyl siding of the house
where she lived.

There was nothing to mourn.

Visit

My doctor speaks staccato—
looking up every few sentences.

His dim office
like a 24 hour diner
where waitresses
pinch the salt
off french fries
and black leather booths smile
with cigarette burn dimples.

A photo of a Dalmatian
hangs crooked over me.
Spots like oil spills—
missionary marks
on an orca's back.

He encourages
cohabitation.
Live with another
and forget where you fray.

I tell him I live
with the ghosts
of vengeful past lovers.
He nods and agrees
it's a start.

On the walk home
my umbrella exhales
inside out.
And the rain stops
as quickly as it began.

At the pharmacy
I fill my prescription
and chew rose petals
like a starving romantic.

Live with another.
Time's too short.

Bury a lover's jawbone
and hope to grow an apple tree.
My doctor would be proud.

I am making progress.

II.

Bloom

"You might see a rose, but never the perfume."

—Arthur Miller

Other Seasons

In summer
    I stumbled through her room.
Growled and carouselled
    to match her ballet steps.
I grinned
    like a bashful hyena.

    In autumn
I sang into her mouth.
I knelt in prayer.
    I got saved.

In spring
I'll find love beneath the deck
    where the pill bugs thrive.
I'll find love
under her eyelids—
    some dark place.

    In winter I'll etch her name
into the glassy lake. I'll burrow
in snow and sleep for a century.

It's the little things—
    certainly.
So small
I can keep them
under my tongue.
The blue sparks
that bounce
and hope to catch
    the kindling.

This season
     I'll run my fingers
down the small of her back.
Learn the ridges of vertebrae
where secrets
     are forgotten like worms
          in dry earth.

On Waking

Navigate through heaven's
    half squint. Make coffee
on the stove—naked
      slipping in her footsteps.

Peel back the day.
Tie a centipede
to a balloon string. Excavate
      ripe fruit.

    Something remembered—unwound
across my tongue. A pillow
    shrugs—stillness flickers
        and surrenders.

Smirk like a cracked closet. Reprise
    uncalculated hands. Watch a ceiling
sink to meet you. Listen to the roar
    of trucks in reverse
        and sleep accordingly.

Blond

Pulling a hair from my head
that isn't mine—
blond with a wave
that I can see so clearly
even as my vision warps
    words
and
    words
        warp
            themselves
like sick psychiatrists.

You must've left it
for me (the hair that is)
to inspire a poem about illness.
As you know I hate doctors
and refuse to get better.

Requiem

The herd split.
The furnace consoles
limbs pruned by long showers.
When I remember you

it isn't at all
as I'd hope. It's a piano
detuned. A shadow
big enough to sleep in.

There's sweat buried
in this song. Footsteps
like drums. Only
your hands seem to age.

Now—let the skin
sag and antiquate.
Pregnant in the head
and still dry as a hack.

Bridesmaid

Saw you last night
on a street
I never drive down.
You held your drink
like a rabbit's foot
or a bouquet.

My ring finger
quivered. Your arm
around my waist.
Cold nose in the nape
of my neck.

I want to speak talk show
with you or maybe
braid our daughter's hair.
I want to keep
butterscotch candies
in a hand painted dish.

I almost told you, instead
I said *maybe sometime*.

Maybe when candles count down
and scarecrows close their eyes.
Maybe we'll play charades
or you can drop my ashes
into a frozen Lake St. Claire.

A wedding ring
glints like a glass eye
or a bare, brass flagpole.

Tease your sister
as you flower
her footsteps.
She will never
inhale the past
like car exhaust.

Doe Eyes

A dancer on her day off
sits on a macramé pillow—
speaks with a drawl
I've never heard before.
Her ashes fall on a tapestry
I bought from Goodwill.

She spends the day
in bed—sometimes
counting the rotations
of a ceiling fan.

She rests her wings—
pipe cleaners bent
into spirals.

I get lost in it sometimes
the sprawl of angles
breathing curves.
An iris.

Tonight I'm surely lost—
watching streamers of saliva
run from the mouth of a
deer. Eyes glazed and
basking
in the warmth of headlights.

Sudden Illusion

A tornado on a leash.

You empty out
    your pockets
       and find a dollar bill
with her name on it.

Black boots
    with sharp heels.
A cracked hourglass
and a voice
    like hollow points.

You empty out
your night stand
      and find
    her silver bracelet.

A half shrug folded
in a letter—postage paid
    with a balled fist.
Return address—
    two brittle nails
    sunk into your eardrums.

You empty out
completely. Gauge on E.
    What you had hoped for
isn't at all what it is.

I Wish You The Best

Green sheets that match
    her cheeks. A history
under her breath.
    An empty box
that once contained
    oranges
        rests steadily on the bed.

Candles are lit
    and the smell of lavender
makes my eyes water.

She packs up her things—
    sunglasses
        sanitizers
            wires.

Succulents spring up
    behind her footsteps.
She begins to fade out—
        slow and hypnotic.

    She places the box
    in the back of her car
and I contort my spine.
Still I know
    she can't take it all with her.

Our Garden

The plants have remained unplanted
in their plastic pots
that line the fence between us
and the neighbors we never see.

It was going to be
a vegetable garden as
it's less commitment than dogs
or children but still
something to be proud of
when they grow tall
and reach toward you.

I wouldn't eat anything
that came out of this ground.

A shovel juts from dirt—
claims the land
in the name of an idea
that never quite bloomed.

And though the squirrels
and insects enjoy it—
I still fear one day you'll ask
why we never planted anything.

Mythology

Hide the Polaroid. Your back
pressed against
the blue tiled wall.
One breast covered by blond strands—
draped like lace.

Toenails painted
with ox-blood. The muscles
of your thighs tense.
I would call you goddess
if I still believed.

I feel the weight
of the camera. The smell
of bleach cut
with candle wax.
Silver halide
and the slow reveal.

Years later, in another city
in the bathroom
you hum songs
I never learned
until pupils dilate.

I'd take a picture of that—
your palms blushing
I'd hide that one too.

Madrid to Detroit

I see the city shake
through your sunglasses.

There is a catholic tone
to your letters.

It's the art of remolding history—
turning bricks into Sunday brunch.

Cover yourself in sea salt—
learn the rituals.

Find a fault line
to spread or a timbre of earth.

Everything remains cosmic
in adjustable beach chairs.

In all that I know
I can't always find you.

I wonder if bulls are beautiful
or just sad. If blue is black.

I know red is red.
Even more red.

Thoughts of home are buried
in the back of a suitcase.

A shrine was erected—stuffed animals
on the side of the highway.

The yards are smaller here
but we jump rope with power lines.

Hands move quickly out of the dark
like in a movie you saw in college.

And you'll notice our sunsets
are not nearly red enough.

Space

Asleep in the Russian doll
of rooms—that is—my dream
of sleep. There's still room
for you here.

We meet at a bar
you used to like. That space
between your teeth
still makes me feel quiet.

In your room I sweat
patiently under a white duvet.
I feel sleep close in—
hands over my eyes.

Once we hollow out—
empty our chests and leave
a cavity. That's when
we'll have space for each other.

This room—a temple of satellites.
A nest of fine hair. Is it a room
without space? Four walls silent
and missing children.

Cinema

We talk in 35 millimeter sentences
and a projector hums in the background.

White noise like unexpected tide—
the whirl at the end of the reel

as it falls on a floor older than the devil.
I follow trails under blankets

and bedroom doors. Locust
scrape their legs and knit

a melody—half as pretty
as you in spring. I missed you then.

Collected cobwebs for a fake museum.
I miss you now certain

as a copper clock-hand. A breeze
unheard. You were always musical—

arms bowed like a cello until
you rubbed elbows with me.

And in childhood I touched hands
with you. And you

are the centipede of my dreams—
benevolent on the ceiling

but still crawling to the light
that vanishes under blankets.

I Told You So

The wind blows your favorite baseball cap
into an open sewer grate.

And I think if I were you
I'd fall to my knees in perfect melodrama.

Instead you walk quickly
to the side door—carrying cat food.

You've never mentioned the hat
but I imagine you think about it.

Sometimes I feel so happy to know you.
Other times I'm glad I don't.

Barbs

I.

There's a woman
named Barbara.
Her hair floods into kitchen sinks
and piles up in shopping malls.
Her eyes are half open
in the dark—oil slicks
and fade-outs.

She writes two line poems
more like jokes. One goes—
*I find solace in those
who look for it.*
And she pins them
to her fridge
with tacky magnets.

She's been to every city
and there's a scar
just under her lip
from a softball.

She doesn't drive except
in a dream she once had.
She was a train conductor
though it was only a toy train
on a track
made out of toothpicks—
though it was only a dream,
Barbara.

She carries change for pay phones
that don't exist anymore.
She says she's half-Jewish
but talks about God most often
turn into talks about childhood.

She brings me wine on occasion
from a vineyard in France
that she went to once with her family.
I can't tell the good from the bad—
and the bad is often
my head in the toilet
and Barbara in the living room
carving a bird into the coffee table
with a jeweled switchblade.

She once had plans to fling herself off a roof
and I asked which one.

II.

I can count her on one hand.
Barbara—
     where have you left me now?

Barbara, I'm nauseous. Barbara,
the kitchen smells like rotten fruit
and all I can taste is chalk dust.

Barbara, is it Friday yet?
I need a check to cash.
I wanna go downtown
and ride the elevators all night.
Yes. Yes. Yes.

Barbara, I can't go
to the East coast.
What if there's another hurricane?
What if I like it there
and don't want to come back?
Or even worse—
what if you like it there.

Barbara, ask me
what I'm thinking.
Barbara, I want to quit
and be rich. I'll see Singapore

with you, Barbara.
You haven't seen Singapore yet—
have you?

Barbara, with freckles
like birds' feet. In child's tongue
Bar-bar-a. Smiling
into your wrists.

Barbara, I think
that in your dream
I'm tied to the tracks
screaming, Barbara.
Plucking at the tiny knots.
I think maybe that's why
you don't drive.

III.

Barbara,
we must rescue each other.
Split the difference.
Indulge and interpret
on Egyptian cotton.

We know our language is false
and our skin holds us back
but we'll bite anything
that will sharpen our teeth.

We must be precious, Barbara—
hanging from a crooked halo.
You take the elevator to the roof
of a building I don't know the name of.

Barbara, sit with me
and forget about birds for a second.

III.

Memory Revisions

"you will go (kiss me

down into your memory and
a memory and memory
i)   kiss me, (will go)"

—e e cummings

Lost Rivers

The drained days
of the week.
Muscles ripe
under gaudy sky.

After work
follow two great rivers
until they meet
and forget themselves.

Life is unrelenting and covetous
of those who do not wish to participate.

Leave nature with the tab.
Drift from dream-state
to dream-state. Offer
old songs as repayment.

Gather advice from
crumpled napkins.
Wash yourself clean
in the misting river.

The past is religion and you
are the patron saint of forgetting.

Dinner Time

A house fly glitters
in a bowl of rice.

A skeleton waves
romantically.

Around six o'clock
you boil Leviticus

with kidney beans.
A bell rings like the sound

of breaking china.
Your father runs his fingers

down his belt
and sniffs the air

for the scent of dying cells
or boys.

Baby Teeth

Girl stares grimacing
at the syringes
dipped into sunny pores.
Rays outstretched
to the edges of sobriety.
A convert—
she's non-practicing.

Poached eggs
in the ashtray—watch
girl pick up
the split shells
of her father's pistachios.

She gnashes her overbite
at the crumbs and dust and shit.
Nestled in the crook
of a lawn chair—
he nods
and scratches his belly.

She licks cracked light bulbs—
kiss practice.
Girl rests in a truck bed
full of pigs feed.
At night she pretends
not to hear the squealing.

Her brother drowns mice
in a china pot of warm milk.
A brown bag veil—
Dionysus on his tongue.
He slithers on the patio
and mumbles his vertebrae
into a winking coma.
Girl catches prey
in fishnet stockings.

Girl muzzles her hands—
hacks with gusto.
Life is an uppercut
motherfucker
she cranes into the receiver.

As they watch television
a preacher caught in his own hysteria
dangles an infant from a window.
Girl stares grimacing—
gumming a lollipop.

Weekends

I.

A Sunday is spent
in a cramped backseat.

I sit and watch the sunrise
on a gin soaked blanket.
I thank God
for the thanks I get
in straw and silk
and all the ants in between.

I keep the neighbors up.
But if my pen
made more noise
I'd spend less time fucking.

The car doesn't run
so I live a Sunday
on borrowed time.

I pile hay
in needle stacks.

I breath a bellow
and speak
with flecks of sesame seeds
in my teeth.

In this house—
hamburgers and aspirin.
Grapevines grow
from my calves
and sharks feast
never full.

A Sunday stares ahead
and sees snow—
or maybe
the sticky substance
of humility—

honey mixed with salt.
Sex without words.

Mixed up as it might have been
I've never forgotten.

II.

I paint my illness
in gas station bathrooms
across the country.

I misspell amphetamines
and play the harp
in muted chords.

I rip the knockers off doors
and hope no one will hear.

She regurgitates
bank receipts.
A prominent nose
slightly bent
—like the end of a cigarette.

Nothing changes
until it's flung against a wall
or fucked without smiling.

She asks if I know
that place.
The one of reptile blood
and scales.

The cruelty of a tribunal.
The curse of reputation.

She asks if I know
the weight of a ripe heart.

I nod
and the camera pans
to the hot breath
that sticks to train tracks.

Fiddlestick

Hope to be
    beaded heart
        and fiddlestick.
An accident and a curse.

      Find the message
          in a cascade of tomato
paste. Burn
    bite
        and bury
        your effigies.

Make plaster casts
    of broken noses.
            Make a mess of the coastline—
            the bust of a nation.

Fall hopelessly in love
    with your mistakes

           and wait for them to leave you too.

Underpinnings

This day has been
a pregnant mother
spun by her braids.
Toppling like a hard-boiled
Easter egg.

This day has caught
a bullet
in the mouth.

I thought of her today
moving like a pheasant
through traffic.

The warmth of her palms
and the backs
of her knee caps.

The day continued—
a well deep
but dry.

A day of still air
and alligator breath
and suddenly
you're up to your ankles
in blue-black muck.

It's the underpinnings.
Monthly rain
like blood
that stains shoes
and plants alike.

The day that grows
legs and red high heels
and stampedes
across the chests
of antlered men.

Funnel-Vision

Curiosities found
in the attics
of long dead relatives.

The sins of dog owners.
Self-flagellation
for walks untaken.

Light sucked from a room
and replaced with nothing
not even darkness.

Vision spirals in—
lightning bugs
drunk in spring.

Agoraphobe

In a heat that curls
refrigerator magnets
a magenta sun
segues me into 2D.

Voices hide their tune.
They settle in
stingray nets and
major keys.

In the fossilized remains
of wall clocks
and watches—
I feel ancestors breathe.

I've tried to learn
patience from numbers
or the braille
of knuckles.

In the heat
and in your voice
I can remember
almost nothing.

A revision of the past.
A room I never left.

Summer Sick

You age quickly
in the heat.
Roots shrivel
around your ankles.

You drink water—
though mostly beer
when it's too hot
to wash dishes
and fingers run circles
around rims
of sticky glasses.

You scoff at rainclouds.
Delirious and dreaming
of central-air.
This summer you smile

as asphalt hisses
a psalm. You speak
and forget whatever
the hell you were saying.

Rust Belt

In the back of a silver Honda
you smirk through an ear infection.
Imagined siblings ask
for your headphones.

Ohio seems to rust
all around you.
Factories and car lots
spill over into your dreams.

There are redactions
in the photo albums.
Someone who isn't me
holds a Mylar balloon

so tightly that his knuckles are white.

Powwow

Very Chuck
Berry. Kinda wild
blues and pinwheeled
eyelids. Smirked
at pesticides. Called you
a wallflower.

You sat
sang songs.
I sang too and watched
a thought bubble inflate
and pop
above your head.

This powwow—
sitting cross-legged
in a convenience store
strumming along
to the muzak.

Attempting to shimmy
for loose coins
or black circles
that never change.

Cloudbuster

In a makeshift
locust/corn husk
kinda voice. I sing
through bleachy mist.

I exaggerate shadows
and burn
through a paycheck
in a day.

Notice the outline
of a frame
that once hung
above the sofa.

The breeze blows
summer back west.

A storm jostles
the heavens
and snaps a tightrope
of power lines.

What I was trying
to say was—
pray for rain
expect a flood.

Now—barefoot.
Drawn to cicadas and bee wings
that glitter.

Plastic in barbed wire.
Nap on the stalagmites
or might-nots
in the buttery rain.

Fodder

I'd rather write
and be well. Blow
smoke rings
into a fireplace.
Turn wine to vinegar—
history to myth.

I'd rather be
the road. The sunken eyes—
rubies in the rain.
I'd sway with traffic lights.
Feel dull as cigar smoke.

Instead I count tiles
              and panels
           and planes
        and planets
    and asterisks
as I channel surf through a dim galaxy.

I'd rather paint
your freckles on my face.
Find somewhere
to stray. Recite Williams
while you're at work.

I'd rather be
the fodder—
the bullet—
the face in the dark.
Something necessary
and still unknown.

Animals

I.

An heirloom locket
    hung by chicken wire.

II.

Anamorphic cartoon characters
on strike.

III.

The dog/God dilemma.

IV.

Microchip ear-tags used
for livestock. The branding
of cattle. Wolves investing
in sheep's clothing.

V.

Eric Arthur Blair turns
in his grave but he's still here
to fight against fascists.

VI.

I'll share what you share
in divisions of madness.
I'll eat what you eat.

VII.

I'm barely housebroken
but looking for a good home.

A Curious Child

On the arches of my heart.
        On the tip of my breath.
                It falls
on
me

to pluck
    bees from flowers
        and brush my teeth
            with antacids.

                        It
                        falls
        out the window
    like a curious child.

On the crest
    of a neuron I order
        the ocean
        from
        McDonalds.

    I pay the rent
        with dirty Kleenex.
I forget my clothes
    and dress in yours instead.

I fled from catechism
    and buried a crucifix
in the backyard.

    Sometimes I shudder
at a wind chime.
    Sometimes I fall
in love.

My future is chrome.
    A finely polished bar rail.

Curious still
    about what
        makes us laugh
alone.

There's a joke
    about God.
    I'd rather not tell. I'm sure
        you're already laughing.

Grand Rapids, MI

I.

An heirloom locket
They bleach the snow here.
Teeth sink in
and we never bite back.
There are no battles
in this town. We're all
extinguished and hissing.

Buildings glint
like steel revolvers.
Western smiles
forget your name
and apologize profusely.

Lucy lets Charlie Brown
kick the football
halfway across the country.

The brides are bored
and fawning over
the flora of Lake Michigan.

We stare at the sky
and think—
        a million other suns
     could be just as lucky.

II.

In an old haunted house
we attempt romance.
Our terrors are realized
and memorized with precision.

I don't know how to talk dirty
anymore.

Only fill in the blanks
and cavities.

    I know how
    to make metal
    crest and curve
    with your collar bone.

III.

A burlap sack
    in the trunk of a Volkswagen.
The crumbs in the back of your wallet.
We're all missing—
    remembered only for our disappearance.

A thin
chalk
outline.

I tried to make time
    where there wasn't.

Chalk up another.

We can meet
in the middle. Reintroduce
ourselves.

    Swat flies off bare shoulders.
Turn truth into posture then
    forget our limbs.

O certainly—
chalk up
another.

The terrors of a city
that will remember your face
and nothing else.

Cardinal Direction

North is not up.
Here—just pine trees
that split words

and beach sand.
If there is a coast
I've missed it

—dial in
a.m. for more snow.

Fortune Telling

The steel wool
    snarls. The green tea
peaks—leaves

loose and cursive line
    the ripples of her hands.

The remains of a porcelain
      coffee mug.
    A smile without eyes
or teeth—just blood. Pine needles
    in the winking drain.

    The taste of copper
like a penny dipped
in morphine. You won't dream
      on that.

Cool drone
    like a spider
        eating a wasp.

    A finger skinning an apple.
Tying the red ribbon of flesh
      in a knot.

Thoughts on Time

I mix up time.
I see clock hands curl
and find white sand
in the pocket
of my winter coat.

I'm not so quick to forget
spit, sweat, bare-feet
on linoleum.
In the kitchen my mother
strokes a butcher knife—
mutters under her breath
God tells bad jokes.

Time is a 65 year-old man
in the driver's seat
of a rumbling truck.
Grease stains
on his bowling shirt.
He's headed to Florida
alone. He's quick
to forget
rusted razor blades
on the bathroom sink,
pillow cases stuffed
with sand, crumpled pages
and more simply
lying flat.

A lover returns a phone call.
Tone is bit-crushed. The line
buzzes fluorescent.
Breath short like a wolf
caught in a trap.

Time groans through traffic—
breaks the radio—smashes
the dashboard with his forehead.

In time you'll hear bursts
of yellow laughter.
Cold static from a bent
antenna. A tame ocean.
A child's nickname.

When I was a child
I spat at the mirror.

I ate birthday cake with my hands.
I thought Time was younger
and drove a coupe.
I mix up time but I'm not
so quick to forget
my creation myths.

In Florida—Time wades calmly
into the ocean. He navigates
the coral and jellyfish and floats
on his back until the tide
pulls him back to shore.
On the phone
silence congeals in my throat.

A lover who'd like to be
smooth steel—bred
from bullets
and flame.
She's not so quick
to resist
prying fingers
at triggers—
the spider asleep
in his web. Blood
on her bedsheets. A heavy
stone. Wobbling dominoes.
Anyone
who knows.

A lover lets me down
and Time trips on
a sandcastle.

I'm not so quick
anymore. Just a snake
praying in the garden.

ACKNOWLEDGMENTS

Infinite thanks and praises to my parents, friends, family, and strangers whom without, this book would never exist. 11:11 Press, Andy, and James for their unwavering support and tireless efforts. Colleagues, mentors, teachers. My compatriots of the 51 West Warren Writers Workshop. The city of Detroit and all past and fictitious lovers. Thank you.

ABOUT THE AUTHOR

Photo by Evans Tasiopoulos

Vincent James Perrone is a writer and musician from Detroit, Michigan. He is a winner of the Christopher T. Leland Scholarship in Creative Writing and former Editor-in-chief of the Wayne Literary Review.

About the Publisher

11:11 Press is an American independent literary publisher based in Minneapolis, MN. Founded in 2018, 11:11 publishes innovative literature of all forms and varieties. We believe in the freedom of artistic expression, the realization of creative potential, and the transcendental power of stories.

www.ingramcontent.com/pod-product-compliance
Lightning Source LLC
Chambersburg PA
CBHW020127130526
44591CB00032B/564